GET THE F$#% UP OUT OF HERE

A Comedic, Reflective Journey Through Transitions That Will Save Your Sanity and Create a Safety Net of Success

PUBLISHED BY: Melodie J. Kent

GET THE F$#% UP OUT OF HERE:
A Comedic, Reflective Journey Through Transitions That Will Save Your Sanity and Create a Safety Net of Success

First Edition, 2026

ISBN: 978-0-9826621-2-0

For permissions, please contact:
juvelwc@gmail.com

Disclaimer:
This book reflects lived experiences and personal reflections. All stories told with humor and truth for personal development and growth. If you experience severe distress or symptoms affecting daily life, please consult a qualified mental health professional.

DEDICATION

To my seeds, Moné, Isaiah, and Jai, and my sweet grandchild, Zen—

You are the truest part of my story. Each of you carries a piece of my heart, my hope, and my healing.

This book is for you.

Because one day, you'll face transitions too—some loud and disruptive, some quiet and necessary. And I want you to know that change doesn't mean the love was wasted. It just means the chapter was complete.

You have given me purpose when I felt lost, joy when I felt empty, and strength when I didn't think I had any more to give.

So let this book be your compass when the world gets confusing.

Let it remind you that you are allowed to choose joy, to walk away from misalignment, and to move with dignity—even when it's hard.

Because just like this book, you are a legacy in motion.

"Sometimes letting things go is an act of far greater power than defending or hanging on."

— **Eckhart Tolle,** *A New Earth*

TABLE OF CONTENTS

ACKNOWLEDGEMENTS

Before anything else—thank you, God, for the journey, the covering, and the clarity to see it through.

To my parents, **Phillip Kent Sr. and Jan Kent**—thank you for being my number one supporters from day one. You have been the backbone of my life. You will never experience richness in love until you've been a child of Phillip and Jan Kent. The way you've poured into me shaped everything I am becoming.

To my children, **Mone, Isaiah, and Jai**—thank you for trusting me with the greatest role I will ever have: Mommy. You love me beyond my faults, and somehow, you always know when I need a warm hug the most. You are my why, my grounding, and my joy.

To **Bliss, Jake, and Kcrots**—I didn't fully understand support until I had you all behind me on this project. From late nights to "mission impossibles" turning into completed tasks, thank you for it all. You are the crew that held me together in more ways than one. Bliss, thank you for trusting me with your closest partners. People don't know what a dream team is until they experience the level of care, concern, and creativity you all bring.

To **Shawn Blanchard**—thank you for your wisdom and guidance. You didn't just create a playbook—you made sure I ran the play. From the emails, to the check-ins, to the feedback, I am forever grateful. Even when there were minor kinks, I never doubted that your wisdom would help me find my way back on track.

To my editing team—**Loretha G., Michelle E., Jonathan B., Mikaheel S., and Matilda**—thank you for your perspectives, your thoughtful pushes, and your constant encouragement. You helped sharpen not just my words, but my message.

To **everyone who poured into me, saw me for my true self, pulled me together like a little Black girl's edges, told me I was still good enough, or simply gave me room to breathe**—thank you. I may not list every name, but please know, from the deepest part of my heart, I am grateful for you. And if I ever have the opportunity to thank you in person, I will make it a priority. Relationships are not easy, so when you find people who stand beside you and recognize that the best version of you is sometimes still waiting to be released—I can get down with those kinds of people. If you know, you know.

And finally, to myself—
Thank you for being courageous.
Thank you for choosing healing and forgiveness.
Thank you for being honest, even when it was uncomfortable.
Thank you for pushing for clarity—because clarity is kindness.
Thank you for finding who you are, and who you refuse to be.
Thank you for not letting perfection be the enemy of progress.

And most importantly—thank you for laughing your way through life…

while still knowing when it's time to say,

"It's time to get the f$#% up out of here."

PREFACE

From the version of me who stayed too long

The Art of the Exit isn't something I believed in.

I believed in staying.
In pushing through.
In making it work—no matter how heavy it felt.

Because that's what I was taught.
Commit. Be loyal. Don't quit.

I wore endurance like a badge of honor.
Even when everything in me was tired.
Even when the quiet voice inside kept whispering,
"This ain't it."

I didn't trust that voice.

I called it fear.
I called it doubt.
I called it everything except what it really was—truth.

Because walking away?
That felt like failure.

And I wasn't raised to fail.

So I stayed in places that drained me.
Held on to things that outgrew me.
Smiled through moments that were slowly breaking me.

And people applauded it.

They called it strength.
They called it commitment.
They called it "doing the right thing."

But deep down… I knew something wasn't right.

What I didn't understand then—what I couldn't fully see—was that sometimes the most powerful move you can make is to walk away.

Not out of weakness.
Not out of impulse.
But out of alignment.

This book?
It's not the version of me who stayed speaking anymore.

It's the version of me who finally listened.

The one who learned that leaving isn't quitting—
it's choosing yourself.

The one who stopped calling endings failures
and started recognizing them as growth.

Through raw storytelling, awkwardly funny moments,
and painfully honest truth, Melodie walks you through transitions
that don't come with a manual.

But more importantly—
she gives you permission.
Permission to reflect.

Permission to question.
Permission to stop holding on to things
that no longer hold you with care.

If you're anything like I was,
you've been taught to stay longer than you should.

To prove your strength through endurance.

To confuse loyalty with self-sacrifice.

But by the time you finish this book,
you'll start to see things differently.

You'll laugh.

You might cry.
But most of all—you'll recognize yourself.

Because this book isn't just a story.

It's a mirror.
A compass.
And a quiet nudge toward the door you've been afraid to open.

And if nothing else,
I hope you walk away knowing this:

The exit door isn't the end.
It's the beginning.

— The version of me who finally learned to get the f$#% up out of there.

HOW TO NAVIGATE THIS JOURNEY

This isn't a spectator sport. You're here because you're ready to move, and this book is the vehicle. Here is how we're going to do this:

The Narrative & The Resonance: Part I is the story. Part II is your space to speak back, resonate, and apply these lessons to your own life.

Journaling The Reflection Corners: At the end of every chapter, stop. Use this space to sit with what you just read.

The Vision Board Section: When you see a prompt, navigate to the Vision Board Section. Use the guide in the back to piece your vision together until you have a full, clear picture of your "Exit."

The Journaling Section: When you see a prompt, head to the Journaling Section in Part II. Write it out—don't just keep it in your head.

The Reality Portal - Your Completed Vision: And finally, at the very end, you'll find a dedicated space to bring your vision board to life. This is where you paste your photos, quotes, and dreams to see the whole picture in one place.

Bottom line is, the transformation isn't in the reading; it's in the doing.

Give yourself permission to be real and messy—that's how the journey actually starts.

INTRODUCTION

The Art of the Exit

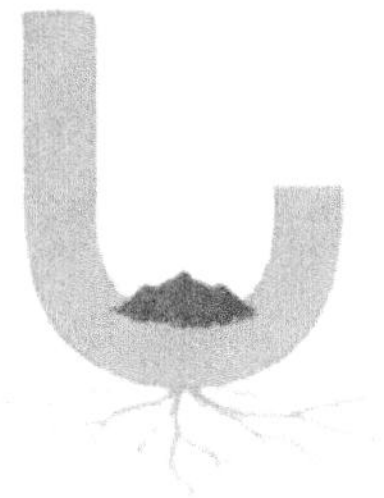

One thing I've learned in this life? There's *always* a time to exit. But the trick—the *art*—is getting the timing just right.

Leave too soon and you'll ache. Stay too long and it'll break you. But when you hit that sweet middle—where you've outgrown the space, but haven't let it consume you? That's the art of the exit. And baby, let me tell you, I've had to learn it the hard, hilarious way.

Every time I needed to go, my body knew before my mouth could say it. My spirit would shift. The humor in me—the thing that usually helped me survive—would slowly vanish. And when I stop laughing? Oh, you better believe something's wrong.

Why do transitions matter?

Because we're taught to stay. For the kids. For the pension. For the title. For the home we "can't sell yet." For the comfort of certainty in a space that's draining our souls. And I've seen too many people— *myself included*—trade vision for obligation. Stay put to keep others comfortable while neglecting ourselves completely.

But here's the truth: if a situation is going to make me lose my peace, my money, my joy—or have me showing up as someone I don't even recognize? *I have to go.*

Period. No debate. No apology. I believe in growth, yes, but I don't believe in mutating into someone unrecognizable just to stay where I don't belong.

That, my friend, is the art of transition—and trust me, it's not just about jobs or zip codes.

Transitions Aren't Just Physical

We think of transitions as quitting a job or moving to a new city. But they come in all shapes. You can transition your mindset. You can transition how you show up for others. You can transition how you love, how you parent, how you *believe*.

The fact is, not every transition comes with bold letters and fireworks. Sometimes it sneaks in through the back door, disguised as ordinary life. Those smaller pivots may look minor, but they're often the ones that train us for the heavier shifts ahead.

I didn't realize it then, but even the tiniest changes were teaching me about choice and change—teaching me that transition isn't just about the dramatic, movie-scene moments. It's also about the everyday decisions that quietly reshape how we live.

And in my case, one of the first lessons didn't come from some life- altering event—it came from babies. A lot of babies. What I now call my "From Auntie Overload to Deal or No Deal" season, and trust me, it taught me plenty about shifting when life gets heavy.

I come from a big family—big in love, big in laughter, and *prolific* in procreation. My mama had five kids, and once those babies got grown, they *multiplied* like the Lord had personally handed them a fertility coupon.

I was eight years old when I became an aunt. Baby, I thought I was their third parent. I was ready with the wipes, the bottles, and the Barney DVDs (I still can't look at purple without twitching).

But fast forward a bit—I got older, got a little change in my pocket (emphasis on "little"), and decided I wanted to bless these babies with savings bonds. I wanted to be *that* aunt. The one who showed up, gave meaningful gifts, and had her financial house in order. And for a while? I did just that.

Until the number of nieces and nephews started increasing *exponentially*. Not linearly—no, no— *exponentially*. My salary? Very linear. Their births? A geometric sequence on Red Bull.

Come December, I was hyperventilating in Target. The gifts, the guessing games (Is it Barney this year? Blues Clues? Paw Patrol?), the money—all of it. And one day, I just *snapped*.

I looked at my budget and said:
"Y'all, I love y'all… but I can't be Santa, the North Pole, and the reindeer too."

So I transitioned.

At first, I turned to raffles. They were simple, fun, and most importantly, they kept me on budget. When the family walked in the door, I'd hand out raffle tickets like it was Saturday at H-E-B—our local Texas grocery store where folks line up for free samples and good gossip.

And just like those sample counters, some folks doubled back trying to sneak another ticket. I'd catch them, call them out, and laugh, because I understood: the anticipation of winning can make anybody a little dishonest.

I'd fan fresh bills in the air, taunting the crowd with holiday cash. A kid always drew the winning ticket— tiny fingers digging deep in the bag, bouncing with excitement, while grown folks whispered bribes in their ears. I milked every moment, reading numbers slowly, tension building until somebody hollered like they'd just been baptized. Winners shouted, losers yelled "cheater," and the whole room cracked up.

Those raffles filled me with so much joy that eventually, I wanted more. That's when the game shows were born. Thus: *Deal or No Deal—Family Parody Edition.*

It wasn't just a raffle anymore; it turned into a full production. I built a tri-fold board, just like I did back in science fair days. Dollar store decorations, printed photos, family stickers, lights—the works. Each photo became a "suitcase," and inside was a denomination from one penny to $150.

When a player picked a suitcase, I sat them front and center. Lights flashing, faces grinning from the crowd, and me— playing the banker. One by one, they picked, holding out hope that $150 stayed alive. I stretched the suspense, raised an eyebrow, even offered "banker deals" in my slickest Wall Street voice.

Kids squealed, grown folks hollered, and the whole house roared like it was prime-time TV. But here's what really changed: *for the first time, giving didn't feel like losing.*

Was it hard to transition at first? Absolutely. People talked. Called me cheap. Judged my decision. But now? It's tradition. Over a decade strong. Every year, I create memories with my family through new games and adventures—without sacrificing my mental health or financial stability.

This Book is About That Kind of Shift

Sometimes transitions are seismic—divorce, layoffs, relocation. Sometimes they're subtle—shifting expectations, reclaiming boundaries, redirecting energy. Over the last decade—from my greatest leadership leap in 2016 to launching Juve in 2022—this book traces every shift that taught me how to leave well and live free.

This is my story of exits, re-entries, and reinventions— from toxic jobs to marriage, from shifting my wealth mindset to laughing through stress with my family. I'll walk you through how I knew when to leave, how I made peace with the fallout, and how I found myself again on the other side.

In the chapters ahead, we'll cover work, love, money, and leadership. And between chapters, I'm going to make you pause—yes, *you*—to check your own transitions.

And before we dive into those exits and entrances, I want to show you, the anchor that's kept me steady through every shift. Because no matter how wild the transition, I always had one thing pointing me forward: my vision board.

VISION IN MOTION: THE BOARD THAT BUILT ME

Transitions aren't abstract ideas—they're lived, felt, messy. My vision board became the proof that what you dare to picture, you can step into. Before we dive into the exits and entrances that shaped my life, I want to share the anchor that's carried me through every shift: my vision board.

It isn't just a cute collage of words and pictures—it's my life map. I made it at a birthday party with my homegirl, cutting and pasting like we were back in elementary school. And the result? It was everything.

It had leadership. Travel. Wellness. Culture. Grace. Veggies. A house. A center. Black. Mind. It wasn't just clippings—*it was a mirror*. For the first time, I could see pieces of myself I hadn't said out loud yet. Laid out in glue and paper, there I was—wanting more, daring to believe more.

When I bought my tiny home, I remember standing in the doorway thinking, "These were the words on my board—and now it's the roof over my head." When I launched Juve Leadership Wellness Center, I felt the same shock—like my scissors and glue had predicted it before I even had a plan.

I dreamed big—and instead of recreating a vision every year, I committed to this one. Until I check off every dream on that board, I won't be adding new ones. That is, unless it aligns with my greater purpose.

This isn't just a goal-setting exercise— it's *alignment in action*. So as you read, reflect, and laugh your way through these transitions, I want you to keep this truth close:

"Your vision is not a wish list.
It's a blueprint. But you have to be bold enough to build."

That board is still hanging, still daring me to move. And now it's your turn. What I learned from my family game nights is this: small choices stack. They may not come with fireworks or applause, but they shape everything.

So here's your turn at the board—no lights, no audience— just you and your next right step.

(No board yet? **Turn to the Vision Board Section (p. 93)** and Jot three images/words that pull you forward right now.)

JOURNALING THE REFLECTION CORNER: YOUR TRANSITION CHECK-IN

Transitions aren't abstract; we feel them. Use this space to get honest, align your vision, and choose one next move—no dissertations, just truth.

Spot the Shift (Name it)

SOUND IT OUT:

What part of your life feels like it's changing (work, love, money, health, identity, faith)? In one sentence, what's the fundamental shift you sense?

SET IT DOWN:

I'm shifting from

____

____

____

____

____

____

to

____

____

____

____

____

____

because

____

____

____

____

____

____

Signals & Boundaries (Read it)

SOUND IT OUT:

What signs keep repeating? (tension, dread, silence, short fuse, headaches, Sunday scaries, etc.) Which boundaries are you breaking with yourself to stay comfortable? Where have you already started saying "no" (even quietly)?

SET IT DOWN:

The signs I'm noticing:

____

____

____

____

____

____

Boundaries I need to reset:

____

____

____

____

____

____

Vision Check-In (Align it)

SOUND IT OUT:

If you have a vision board (physical or digital), which pieces still resonate with you? Which pieces feel like old costume jewelry—pretty, but not you anymore? What has already manifested, and how did it feel when it did?

SET IT DOWN:

Still Aligned:

____

____

____

____

____

____

Ready to retire:

____

____

____

____

____

____

When manifestations became real, I felt:

____

____

____

____

____

____

One Micro-Move (Do It)

SOUND IT OUT:

What is one small, low-drama step you can take in the next 72 hours that honors the shift?
Example: one email, one boundary script, one hour blocked, one application, one conversation.

SET IT DOWN:

In the next 72 hours, I will

When/Where:

Support I need:

Self-Permission (Claim it)

Write a single sentence you can read out loud when fear gets loud.

I have permission to:

____

____

____

____

____

____

Navigate to the Journal Section (p. 103) to bridge the gap between your initial visual aspirations and your internal reality, allowing your written reflections to give voice to the images you've curated. Use your journal space to synthesize your past lessons with your future intentions, transforming your vision into a grounded, actionable narrative.

CHAPTER I

That Job That Looked Good On Paper

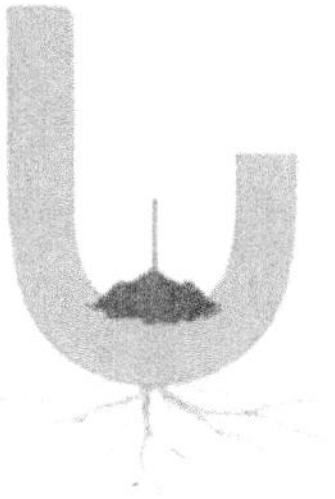

Some jobs look real good from the outside—benefits, proximity, title, even that emotional pull of coming home. But whew, once you step in, the picture ain't always as pretty.

Let me take you back.

I was fresh out of IBM, transitioning from a technical career that kept me on the road. I had just gotten married and wanted to be present in my relationship— not hopping from city to city. So I wrapped up my time in corporate and stepped into teaching. My dad was thrilled. Coming from a family of educators, he saw it as a full-circle moment.

He even introduced me to my new principal, who already knew me. See, I was returning to my alma mater—the place where I walked the halls as a student. Now, I was back with a new last name, a new purpose, and a new path: the classroom.

On paper? It was perfect.

In reality? *Whew, child.* (Yes, child—with a "d." because this job had me aging in dog years.)

I was newly married, pregnant with my first child, and standing in front of a classroom for the first time— completely overwhelmed. I'd gone from being a structured, top-performing student in a magnet program to teaching in a general education classroom where students didn't learn or behave in the same way I had.

I came in thinking I'd change lives on day one. Instead, I was just trying to make it to lunch without crying in my locked classroom. My expectations were unrealistic—not just for the job, but for the kids.

And it was breaking me.

Most days, I'd come home, drop my bag, and go straight to bed. My feet ached from standing, my voice was hoarse from teaching, and my spirit sagged under the weight of trying to motivate kids who couldn't care less about my "new teacher energy."

The tears would roll, blurring the ink on ungraded papers. My arms would fling up in surrender—not because I didn't care, but because I cared *too* much. I wanted so badly to reach these students, but I didn't yet have the tools. I was giving everything I had, and it still wasn't enough.

Then February came—and with it, a letter from the district. They were offering money to anyone willing to commit early to not returning the following year. At first, I thought, *why would they pay someone to quit?*

But then it clicked: they lose more scrambling for teachers in August than planning ahead. And baby, let me tell you—they could've offered me a single dollar, and I would've signed. I marched that paper back faster than you could say *exit interview.*

That was my first authentic taste of the power of choosing to leave.

After that, I spent two years working from home— teaching online, tutoring, dabbling in real estate, breastfeeding between meetings, learning how to build a business and a family. That "break" taught me how to breathe again.

It also taught me something else: I could navigate chaos and still come out whole. The fact that I could breastfeed with one hand while closing a real estate deal with the other told me I wasn't just surviving—I was *reclaiming* my strength. From running a homeschool program to tutoring across the city to juggling side hustles, I was climbing out of the hole I'd dug.

My exit from the classroom wasn't the end of me; it was the reset that reminded me I was capable of complicated things.

It also whispered something I wasn't ready to admit yet: maybe education still had a space for me—but it needed to look different.

So when I returned to the classroom, I came back as a co-teacher. No full-classroom responsibility. Just support. And I *thrived.* I had space to learn, grow, observe, and build relationships. I made lifelong friends, enrolled in a principal certification program, and started to explore what educational leadership could look like.

The return didn't feel as heavy as the first round. I could push forward in education—even if it meant a slower pace. That year rekindled my love for teaching. I soaked up wisdom from master teachers and realized: I didn't have to do it all to belong in the work.

I was content. And others noticed.

One of the teachers I co-taught with told her new job about me, and that led to an offer—a math leadership role right next door to my kids' elementary school. Same parking lot. I could walk them to class, head next door to work, and pick them up after.

No commute. No daycare. Too aligned to ignore. I took it.

The first year? Incredible. The second? Strong. The third? Heavy. The expectations didn't just increase—they piled on. And with no extra support, it started to feel like oppression. A friend once told me, *"Expectations without support is oppression,"* and that line hit differently.

I was breaking.

No matter how hard I worked or how many hours I poured in, it was never enough. I remember sitting in my leader's office in October, tears running down my face. I wasn't angry. I wasn't bitter. I was done.

At that moment, I barely remember the details—just the silence. Thick. Awkward. Unavoidable. The kind that fills a room like an unexpected fart—soundless but pungent. I looked her in the eye and said, "This was my dream job. I loved being near my kids. I loved leading. But this no longer feels like leadership. It feels like shackles. And I can't do it anymore."

I gave my notice—nine months early. I wanted to leave well.

And wouldn't you know it—toward the end of that notice, I ran into a principal I'd worked with before. She asked if I planned to return the next year.

I said, "Ma'am, I would rather sit at home, stare into an empty fish bowl with no water, no fish, and feed that bowl fictitious pebbles for a fish that doesn't exist, than return to a place where I'm misaligned."

We laughed hard. But behind the laughter was clarity. She offered me a new opportunity, and I took it.

That job saved me—until it was time to leave that one, too. But we'll get to that.

What matters is this: I didn't know what the next chapter held. But I knew what it *didn't*. And that was enough to move.

And when you move, the question becomes: toward what? That was the season I realized misalignment will suffocate you—but vision will resuscitate you. That's where my board came in. It wasn't just paper and glue. It was a reminder that clarity always beats chaos.

VISION IN MOTION:
THE BOARD THAT BUILT ME

Go to the Vision Board Section (p. 93)—and don't just look at it like a collage. Look at it like a mirror. A mirror that doesn't just show where you are but dares you to see where you're going.

SOUND IT OUT:

- *Where in your current work are you pretending everything is fine, but your soul knows otherwise?*
- *Are you performing for others while quietly abandoning yourself?*
- *What would a work life in complete alignment with your values, family needs, and spiritual peace actually look like?*
- *What's one shift—slight or bold—that would bring you closer to a more authentic version of you?*

Your vision board doesn't have to be about luxury. *It can be about freedom.* Sometimes it's not a mansion or a passport stamp—it's a picture of you smiling again.

Allow your spoken reflections to guide the curation of your vision board.

JOURNALING THE REFLECTION CORNER:
Rewrite the Role, Reclaim the You

SOUND IT OUT:

Take a moment to get honest with yourself:

- *In what ways has a job, relationship, or commitment required you to shrink?*
- *What parts of your identity have you lost or buried to survive your current role?*
- *When was the last time you laughed—honestly laughed—at work?*
- *If your future self wrote you a letter today, what would they beg you to stop settling for?*

Use the **Journal Section (p. 103)** to reflect, release, and reclaim. Even if you can't walk away today, you can walk toward something better.

Work that feeds your joy—not just your bills—is possible. You are allowed to pivot. Not because you're weak, but because you're wise enough to know:

It's time to get the F$# up out of here.

CHAPTER II

Sis, He's Not Just a Bad Boss – He's The Problem

Now, I'd like to take you into another part of my journey. It was what I considered, at the time, another dream job. It came right after I looked my former boss in the eye and said, *"This feels like oppression."*

Because here's the thing—I don't mind meeting high expectations.

I'm built for that.

But I need clarity and support. And when both of those are missing? That's when the work starts to feel like chains.

In that previous role, demands piled up daily. Priorities shifted without warning. New initiatives popped up without context or connection to anything already in motion. Everything felt like a fire—and I had no water. Just smoke, sweat, and exhaustion. That, to me, is professional oppression.

So, stepping into this new job? It felt like a release. Like unclenching a fist you didn't realize you'd been holding. I could breathe. I could exhale. I could start fresh with people who got it.

Our first meeting was in a small, quiet coffee shop, and I'll never forget it—the smell of roasted beans in the air, the clatter of mugs in the background, and my shoulders finally falling as if I'd released a long-held breath.

For the first time in months, I wasn't bracing for chaos.

I was just breathing.

I laughed again—real laughter, the kind that bubbles up before you can stop it. Sometimes tears, too, because my new team gave me space to both giggle and grieve. I no longer raced for 5 a.m. callouts or sprinted into buildings trying to hold it all together.

Instead, I got to unpack the weight I'd been carrying.

I learned to push myself not by grinding harder, but by creating space for rest and balance. The chaos of education didn't vanish, but for a small window of time, I had peace. And that peace helped me carve a path for other leaders who were just as tired as I once was.

We were a ragtag crew of three to start. No office, no assigned school site—we met in coffee shops and Mexican restaurants. And baby, we built everything from scratch—our vision, our norms, our values. It wasn't just team-building. It was healing.

We said things like:

"My shine is your shine."
"Feedback is a gift."
"We don't dim to let others glow—we glow together."

And we lived it. Our leader would bring small tokens of gratitude to working lunches—little reminders that said, I see you. I value you.

Once, a teammate led a session solo while I followed the next day. When she finished, the room erupted in feedback and praise. We celebrated her glow instead of competing for the spotlight.

That's what "we glow together" meant—one person's win illuminated the whole team.

Feedback didn't come as a dagger. It came as an offering.

I'll never forget one presentation: I had planned for fifteen minutes—but it ran twenty-six. Afterward, my teammate gently said, "That cut into the reflection time. The participants didn't get to sit with what we gave them."

She didn't shame me. She showed me.

And because we'd already built the trust to handle feedback like that, I didn't bristle.

I grew.

That moment changed how I presented forever. And if one moment could shift me? Dozens of those moments transformed us all.

That kind of feedback empowered us. We grew from three to nine. Then fifteen.

Our work expanded. Our contracts expanded. We expanded.

Because we were aligned. Because our leader saw us— not just as employees, but as people. She knew our wounds and helped us build restoration, not just results.

That old oppressive charter job? It wasn't a waste. It taught me coaching, data systems, and the value of sweat equity. So when I finally stepped into a consulting role instead of a school-based leadership position, I carried empathy with me—and that changed everything.

I earned promotions—several, actually. My leadership capacity stretched beyond what I had imagined. We were doing good work—and it showed.

I became an expert in helping people reclaim work-life balance. Creating psychologically safe spaces for hard conversations. Helping teams grow stronger through open, honest communication. Our small pod of three became a cluster of nine. Then another cluster.

We weren't just a team—we were a movement.

But growth has its price. The intimacy stretched thin. And then it happened: a leadership position opened. We all knew who it should be.

We whispered it during site visits, nodded in agreement, and imagined what her leadership would unlock for us. So when the announcement came, the Zoom room went still. A few glances flickered across the screen. We weren't close enough to speak, but I knew I wasn't the only one whispering under my breath. The silence said it all.

We had just witnessed the wrong person crowned.

The one we all expected? She didn't get the job. They gave it to someone she had trained—a white woman. The air shifted. In my one-on-one conversations before the announcement, I'd already said it plainly: "I don't agree with this decision."

Afterward, they spun a rationale in my ear. I tried to process it, but the words twisted me back into another era. The weight of history pressed in, and for a moment, it felt like time itself hadn't moved. I tucked my hair behind my ear, as if clearing the static would change what I'd heard.

But there was no misunderstanding—just injustice. From there, it unraveled.

I worked under the new leader, but it wasn't the same. I was doing more with less support. I even found myself calling my former boss just to get the clarity my current one couldn't give. Thirty minutes with her accomplished what months of asking above me never did.

Eventually, I voiced my frustration to my boss's boss. And instead of support, I was "let go." Despite my impact. Despite my commitment. Despite the legacy I was shaping.

Bitterness came quickly. My emotions swelled, morphed, doubled back. I didn't know who surpassed Hulk in rage, but whoever she was—she had my face. I didn't mask it, either. I said what I felt.

Direct. Repeated. Raw.

Still, I didn't want to leave. I loved the mission. But I was shrinking.

I lost twenty pounds—not from working out, but from stress and skipped meals. My clothes sagged, patched together with safety pins like a bootleg seamstress job—one I prayed no one would notice.

Each fix disguised the frame, but not the truth: I was unraveling.

My spirit eroded. I'd sit at my computer, tears falling despite my protest—not because the work was hard, but because I couldn't understand why something I once loved suddenly felt unbearable. I gave it all— my ideas, my long days, my creativity, even my peace.

And still, I was weary, toggling between strength and surrender, breathing in bullshit, trying to exhale roses.

When they called to let me go, I went numb. No fight. No tears. Just silence.

But in the quiet, another sound emerged—the whisper of my own voice. The one buried beneath Slack pings, policy decks, and gaslighting. The one saying:

You still have something to give. You just need to give it to yourself first.

From that ending came a beginning. I started my own company.

I won contracts.

I partnered with my former boss—the one who was never truly recognized for her genius.

And I gave her the opportunities she had long deserved.

Some exits are forced. Some exits are overdue. And some exits are divine alignment in disguise.

VISION IN MOTION:
RECLAIMING LEADERSHIP ON YOUR OWN TERMS

Even when the team is growing, even when the mission is meaningful, even when the calendar is packed—if your values aren't honored, the space will feel hollow.

SOUND IT OUT:

- *What version of leadership do you believe in?*
- *When have you seen that version honored?*
- *When have you seen it erased?*
- *If alignment required you to build something that doesn't yet exist, what would you create—and what are you still holding onto that's keeping you from starting?*

Go to the Vision Board Section (p. 93). Add an image, a quote, or a color that represents leadership on your terms. This isn't about climbing the ladder. It's about building a ladder no one thought to make.

JOURNALING THE REFLECTION CORNER:
FROM ALIGNMENT TO EXIT

Reflect on a time when something once fulfilling began to sour.

SOUND IT OUT:

What changed?
What did you try to preserve?
What did you learn from staying?
What did you gain from leaving?

Transitions don't always arrive with clarity. Sometimes they show up in fragments: a skipped meal, a tight chest, a laugh you no longer recognize.

Pay attention. Your body will always tell the truth. And when the truth says it's time—don't wait for permission. Get the F*$# up out of there. And walk into the vision you were always meant to build.

Now, transition to the **Journal Section (p. 103)** to articulate the legacy and life that exist beyond the boundaries of this chapter.

CHAPTER III

I MARRIED WHAT I KNEW, NOT WHAT I NEED

This chapter? Whew. Probably one of the hardest to start— and even harder to finish. Both on paper and in life.

During the latter part of my charter leader days—and definitely into my consulting years—I was attending counseling sessions weekly. For three years straight. Then bi-weekly. Then monthly.

Counseling gave me room to breathe—space to ask why I was in certain situations, how I made decisions, and what came next. I'll say this now: if you can find a counselor who gets your background, who understands your walk, maybe even lived a bit of what you're going through—do it. Counseling was one of the best decisions I've made in my life.

Now, I grew up in the Christian faith. I'm not saying that as a punchline, but for many of us, outside counseling was frowned upon. Folks would think, *"If you're going outside the church, something must be really wrong."*

But let a church elder offer wisdom? Oh, that was *ministry.*

Listen. Prayer is powerful. Sometimes you need perspective, too.

And perspective is what I got. I unpacked everything— family communication, self-image, and even why I felt the way I did about my hair and skin. I didn't walk in wearing trauma like a name tag. I walked in with questions. And I walked in with love—because my parents raised me with it. We didn't have much, but I never felt a lack of anything. They made what we had felt like enough.

Through those sessions—some filled with tears, others with laughter—I began to notice something. Right before I left that toxic-boss job, I told my counselor, *"I think I'm going through a deep, dark depression."*

I was isolating and skipping meals. Avoiding and sometimes numbing with a drink or a smoke. My body was waving red flags I didn't want to see.

Most mornings, I'd drop the kids off and post up at a coffee shop on a cushy loveseat in the corner. The baristas knew my order, like it was printed on the menu: *"Mocha latte with almond milk, cinnamon powder, two pumps of vanilla, whipped cream— right?"* (Why they asked like, it ever changed, I'll never know.) I'd grab my cup, cart my little space heater across the room— Texas summers outside, tundra A/C inside—and settle in. I'd sip slowly, work hard, and seven hours later I'd realize I'd survived the whole work day on one cup of caffeine and a to-do list. I buried myself in responsibility and forgot to care for myself.

At one point, I became dangerously underweight. My face looked sunken. My joy was M.I.A. My counselor saw it—even when I couldn't name it.

Friends saw it, too. On a work trip, after a day full of field laughs, a friend slowed her words like she was carrying something heavy: "Mel, I don't know how to say this, but I'm worried. You've lost so much weight." I cracked a joke to lighten it—*"Chile, the way you dragged that out, I thought you were about to tell me you were dying. I just don't eat."* We laughed, but her concern wrapped me tight, like a greeter's hug at an old Southern church. No matter how I joked, she knew.

After I left that job, I expected relief. But the heaviness lingered. As much as I wanted it to be only work, it wasn't. It was my marriage.

That realization doesn't arrive with confetti. It comes with guilt. With grief. With a pit in your stomach.

My people do marriage. My parents—54 years and counting. My brother and sister-in-law—34 and counting. Aunties and uncles—decades. I've watched folks weather bankruptcy, cancer, heartbreak, and still ride. So in my mind, marriage was supposed to last. Period.

So what was wrong with me? Why couldn't I hack it?

Then a colleague said the line that freed me: *"Mel, I married what I knew. Not what I needed. And I didn't know what I needed when I got married."*

Whew. If that ain't a word.

Because my ex-husband is a good man. Strong-minded. A hustler. Funny. A family man who introduced himself by telling me about his daughter. A protector. He reminded me of my dad, my brothers. Like I had welded the men I knew into one person.

That's what I married—home.

But the distance never left. Even when we were together, I felt far from myself. Counseling made me face that truth. And part of that truth included exploring my identity—my desires, my questions about sexuality I'd been too scared to say out loud. I hadn't acted on anything, but the curiosity itself was enough to shift me.

My counselor didn't flinch. Didn't preach. She leaned in. Helped me face what I needed.

Back at home, he asked, *"Do you like me? Is it me? Is it something else?"* I didn't have the words yet. But once I stopped shoving my thoughts down and started naming them, I knew I had to be honest—with him and with myself.

Letting go would take courage.

Around that time, I told my friend—half real-estate agent, half manifester—*"I want a she-shed on an acre."* She laughed, but she believed me. She was on a roll that year, finding homes for four people in my circle, and she promised she'd find mine too.

When an old shotgun house on an acre popped up, I knew. I toured it, had it inspected, placed the bid—then told my husband, "The loan's in my name, but they'll need you on the deed to close.

Will you come?"

He obliged without a fight. I think we both understood: the house was saying what we were too tired or too afraid to say.

On the drive to the title company, I pitched it as a leadership retreat space—because the house wasn't ready for move-in, and my courage wasn't prepared either. But then the work began.

I rolled up my sleeves and got to work. For every wall I took down and every room I opened, something in me opened too. Brushstroke by brushstroke, nail by nail, I could feel my insides catching up to my outsides.

Our little town's slogan is "Country living in the city," and they weren't lying. Mornings came with animal chatter, railroad horns, and wind whistling through the oaks. That soundtrack pulled my spirit into a quiet place. Then I'd drive back to manicured lawns and cul-de-sacs, and the contrast would knock the breath out of me. I stood between two worlds, wondering which one was home.

At some point, the renovation became a crossroads: stay and deny who I'd become, or leave and rebuild while honoring what had been.

Eventually, I told him, "I think it's time we separate." No yelling. No slammed doors. Just truth.

Because truth was—we weren't rekindling. We were existing.

Co-parenting. Co-habitating. But not co-living.

And y'all, I once said I wanted 88 years of marriage. Eighty-eight. But at year 13, I knew:

I didn't have 75 more years in me.

We separated physically. Then emotionally. Then legally. Hardest decision of my life. Also—the most freeing.

For the first time in a long time, I felt whole. Seen. Not just by others—but by myself.

That tiny house carried me. It reminded me I could rebuild and come home to myself.

Even if it looks like a shotgun house on the edge of town. Even if it sounds like the quiet after goodbye.

Even if it means letting go of the 88 years you once planned. Because sometimes… that's how you finally come home to yourself.

And coming home to yourself doesn't happen all at once. It happens in whispers—tiny nudges that say, *this isn't it,* or *you're not okay.* Sometimes it looks like a joke you once made about a she-shed. Sometimes it seems like a wall half-painted, or a breath you didn't realize you'd been holding.

My tiny house was never just wood and nails. It was proof that rebuilding your space can mean rebuilding your soul.

VISION IN MOTION:
Coming Home To Yourself

Disclaimer: This is my personal journey, not clinical advice. If you need support, seek out a licensed professional.

Some visions don't start with clarity—they begin with a whisper. A tug that says, "This isn't it."

A nudge that says, "You're not okay."

A dream that feels like a joke at first, until it becomes your freedom plan.

That tiny home wasn't just a structure. It was a symbol. A womb. A reclamation. And every time I swept the floor, hung a curtain, or patched a wall—I was rebuilding myself too.

Now it's your turn.

SOUND IT OUT:

- *What vision has been quietly calling your name?*
- *What dream have you been laughing off because it feels "too different" or "too far"?*
- *What version of peace have you delayed because it doesn't look like what you were taught to want?*

Go to the Vision Board Section (p. 93). Add a word, an image, a song lyric—whatever pulls you toward your next place of becoming.

This is your blueprint. Not for what others expect of you, but for who you're allowed to be when no one else is scripting your life.

You don't have to explain it. You just have to claim it.

When I finally admitted my marriage wasn't working, it wasn't just about walking away from a person—it was about walking away from an idea I'd been loyal to. That's the most challenging part. We don't just cling to people; we cling to roles, expectations, and identities we've outgrown. The real question is: what are you still holding that no longer holds you?

JOURNALING THE REFLECTION CORNER:
The Marriage You're Still Holding

Take a moment to reflect—not just on romantic partnerships, but on any long-standing role, commitment, or identity you've been married to.

SOUND IT OUT:

- *What have I outgrown but still wear, as if it fits?*
- *Where have I been more loyal to the idea of something than the reality of it?*
- *When was the last time I felt fully myself in this space?*

SET IT DOWN:

I've been showing up as:

____

____

____

____

____

____

But what I need now is:

____

____

____

____

____

____

I'm ready to release the expectation that:

____

____

____

____

____

____

____

____

and replace it with the truth that:

____

____

____

____

____

____

____

____

Your Reflection:
Now it's your turn. Pause. Breathe. Listen.

SOUND IT OUT:

- *Where in your life have you been performing instead of being?*
- *What roles are you holding onto out of obligation—not alignment?*
- *What does peace look like for you—not your mama, not your friends, not society, but you?*

SET IT DOWN:

Write it out below. No filters. No edits. Just the truth.

I am currently carrying:

I am learning to release:

I want to make space for:

Peace, for me, feels like:

____

____

____

____

____

____

____

____

A Gentle Reminder:

Transitions are tender. They crack you open so your truth can breathe. Don't rush the healing. Don't judge the pace. Trust the unfolding.

Your next chapter is calling. And it's not asking for perfection—just permission.

Carry that momentum into the **Journal Section (p. 103)**. Release the old roles; articulate the new you.

CHAPTER IV

The Money Lie They Sold Us

Let's talk about the lie—the one wrapped in a pension, a paycheck, and a pat on the back. The one that says if you stay loyal—loyal to the job, faithful to the grind, loyal to the title— you'll be safe.

I grew up in a household that valued loyalty to work. In our family, job stability wasn't just the dream—it was the definition of success. My principal growing up was at the same school for fifty years.

My dad? Over thirty.

My mama? Same district, same commitment.

My aunt and uncle both retired after decades with the same companies.

The message was clear: stay long enough, and freedom will greet you at the finish line—with a Social Security check and a retirement party.

A finish line covered in confetti and casseroles. If the chips aren't stale, it's only because Auntie refilled the bowl.

Meanwhile, your blood pressure is high from years of stress and silence. And the cake—delicious today—can't sweeten a life that forgot balance. If you aren't careful, your own celebration might take you out right at the finish line.

Through my previous marriage, I saw something different.

Everybody on his side owned something.

They had businesses—bars, cabs, rentals. Not all of it was neat or polished, but it was theirs. I can still see it—dusty floors, crooked shelves, and the sharp soundtrack of *"cho!"* and bumboclaat curses flying from the heated table games, spilling right out the raised windows of that bar-turned-corner store.

Although it was still under construction in some areas, it was theirs to develop and manage. No one told them when to open, how to serve, or who to be. The freedom was intoxicating.

Ownership gave them choices. And that changed something in me. That's when I realized: exiting isn't only leaving a job. It's going back to an old definition of security—one rooted in ownership, not obedience.

It's the art of moving your loyalty back to yourself.

I started to realize that the "security" I'd been raised to chase was... fragile. All it took was one decision in a boardroom, and your safety net vanished.

So I shifted. I stopped treating a W-2 (U.S. employee tax form) like a wedding ring. And when I opened a Roth (a tax- advantaged retirement account), I didn't do it as a wish—I did it as a system.

One of my first mentors during an engineering internship told me, *"I don't care what title you get—the one thing you must own is property."* At twenty, I bought a small duplex, lived in one unit, and rented the other. That rent helped cover my expenses while I was in school.

I was a landlord before I could legally rent a car.

And that wasn't my only stream. Over time, we:

- **Flipped cars** from auction—learned margins, titles, and patience.

- **Ran a snowball truck** in the summers. My ex followed the kids' games around town—teaching them money, business, and how to serve with a smile (and extra syrup if Mama said yes). One August Saturday, the line snaked past the bleachers. Kids sticky, parents grateful, us dog-tired—and proud. Profit? Modest. Lesson? Priceless: we could make money and memories at the same time.

- **Dabbled in trucking**—at one point, three rigs hauling cross-state. Break-even some months, upside down others; always a masterclass in logistics and risk.

- **Tutored, led workshops, and hosted instructional sessions** from the comfort of my living room.

- **Consulted** under my LLC—turning what I knew into invoices with my company's name at the top.

Every stream taught me something—sometimes strategy, sometimes survival. But together, they taught me a big lesson: this isn't just about money. It's about ownership—of time, of choices, of *me*.

Not just of property, but of possibility.

Because here's the quiet truth no one prints on the HR brochure: you are one meeting away from a new org chart. One policy away from a new life.

I've seen it. You wake up, put on your good clothes, spritz the expensive perfume, and walk in smiling—only to be greeted by security at the door, so *no scene is caused* as you pack your livelihood into a printer-paper box. If you're lucky, they give you the lid to cover the shame they created. That's the day I stopped outsourcing my safety—and started building exits on purpose.

While they were coaching me to be loyal to the company, I began learning to be faithful to myself.

Now, I still believe in strategy. Keep the job if it serves your season—learn everything you can. But let it be *one* stream, not the whole ocean. Build a system that loves you back. Build streams not just for income, but for exits—tiny doors you can open before the house catches fire.

Make stability your baseline and freedom your plan.

From my experience, here's what I want you to know:

- Start small and **start where you stand**—skills you already possess can be leveraged into paid work under your own name.

- Let your W-2 be a **training ground**, not a cage. Turn what you learn into invoices later.

- Select streams that align with your **values and capabilities**.

- Hustle is not a personality; **sustainability is.**
- Measure success in **options and peace**, not only profit.

Some months were break-even (hello, trucking repairs at 2 a.m.). Some months covered a mortgage note. All of them bought me options—and options are a kind of peace.

As I moved through different streams, my confidence took on a new shape. Ownership made me more decisive, more spacious. I was less afraid of a "no," because I wasn't asking one place to be my everything.

So when people ask, "How do I create wealth?" I say: You stop looking at wealth as just a salary and start seeing it as a system.

You stop waiting for someone to hand you freedom and start building it.

You stop confusing loyalty to a company with loyalty to yourself.

A note before we go on: This is my personal story, not financial advice. Your path will be your own—consider consulting a licensed professional if you need guidance for your specific situation.

VISION IN MOTION:
REDIFINING WEALTH ON YOUR OWN TERMS

Not all wealth is financial. Some of it is time.

Some of it is freedom. Some of it is peace.

And yes—some of it is money, and you deserve to earn and grow it without guilt.

SOUND IT OUT:

- *What would wealth look like if you didn't limit it to a paycheck?*
- *What parts of your vision need funding—not permission?*
- *How can your current season (or job) train you to fund your dream later?*

Go to the Vision Board Section (p. 93). Add one word or image that represents freedom without fear—the version of your financial future built by you, not just for you.

This isn't about replacing one hustle with another. It's about aligning your hustle with your healing.

JOURNALING THE REFLECTION CORNER: WEALTH WITHOUT THE LIE

Let's get honest. The lie they sold us is heavy. We're not carrying it anymore.

SOUND IT OUT:

- *What beliefs about money no longer serve you?*
- *Where have you traded "security" for silence?*
- *What definition of wealth actually aligns with your joy, values, and vision?*

SET IT DOWN:

I used to believe wealth was:

____

____

____

____

____

____

____

Now I define wealth as:

____

____

____

____

____

____

____

One income stream I've outgrown is:

____
____
____
____
____
____
____

A *vision-aligned* stream I want to build is:

____
____
____
____
____
____
____

Final charge

You are allowed to rewrite your money story. You are allowed to be both stable and free.

That's not a contradiction—that's wealth.

And you are allowed to dream bigger than one paycheck—as a practice in the art of exit from single-income dependence and loyalty-as-identity.

The art of the exit begins with a single thought. Turn the page to the **Journal Section (p. 103)** and answer this: What part of your 'money story' are you officially leaving behind today?

CHAPTER V

ARTIFICIAL INTELLIGENCE, REAL EFFICIENCY

Let me tell you something. When I was out here chasing financial freedom—building my streams of income through consulting, my W-2, collaborations, and community work—I found myself slowly drowning. Not because the work wasn't good, but because the *time* wasn't enough.

I was building financial wealth, yes. But I was also building knowledge wealth—learning from everyone I collaborated with.

And then there was something else: positional wealth. I was sitting at tables with people who might not have cut me a check directly but had the power to unlock opportunities I wasn't going to find just by grinding solo.

Some folks call that *human capital.*

For me, it was proof that wealth is bigger than what sits in your account.

Wealth looks different for everybody. Some people want ten-bedroom houses and Rolls-Royces. Some folks want to live in the same home they grew up in—even after they become millionaires. That's peace to them. A friend once told me about two different "freedom numbers"—one for living comfortably and one for complete autonomy. That second number? That's the one that lets you work when you want—*if you want.* That's the one I'm aiming for.

But here's the truth: you can't build an empire if your systems are stuck in survival mode.

I had too many moving parts—being a parent, a wife, a business owner, a team lead, and an employee. Every role came with paperwork, logistics, meetings, emails, invoices, lesson plans, and deadlines. It was too much. And I couldn't afford a full-time assistant or a team of five.

Then came artificial intelligence. And baby, let me tell you—it changed my life.

Picture this: two people get into a car accident. One calls their daddy, who happens to be a judge. The judge tells them exactly what to do—calm, clear, covered. The other person? They call their grandma—loving, overwhelmed, unsure. That's the gap AI helps close. AI is the judge in your pocket. The strategist on call. It's not perfect, but it levels the playing field.

I could take a picture of an accident, drop a description into ChatGPT, and ask, *"Who's at fault here based on the details?"* Even if the answer wasn't legally binding, it gave me language. It gave me the next steps. It gave me peace in the chaos. And for someone like me, juggling roles, responsibilities, and expectations, that's power.

Emails that once took two hours now take five minutes with the right prompt and a little editing. Team planning? Drafted before my coffee got cold. Lesson plan skeletons, workshop agendas, even recipes with my daughter—done in seconds. One day, I was drafting a tricky email, and the next, I was helping my son study while I was on the road. That flexibility was the breakthrough.

AI became my assistant, my clarity coach, my five-person team. And look, it wasn't always in my voice. I still had to tweak it. But it gave me a *start.* And when you're juggling as much as I was? A strong start is more than half the battle.

Some people call using AI "cheating." I call it *choosing peace.* Because at some point, you've got to ask: why are you still doing it the hard way when the smart way is right here? I wasn't trying to prove I could do it all anymore. I was trying to protect my energy. That was time I could spend laughing with my kids, resting my mind, or dreaming bigger.

That's the real flex—time.

It wasn't just a tech upgrade. It was a mindset shift. My spirit already knew it was time to move differently, but my mind resisted the change, clinging to the old way. That's why so many of us stay stuck—still working with outdated tools, clinging to habits that drain us, and wondering why it all feels so heavy.

When I finally let go of the shame and leaned into the tool that was literally made to help me? I felt unstoppable.

AI didn't replace my grind—it gave me access. It gave me language when I didn't have the words, steps when I didn't have a map, and confidence when all I had was chaos. And when more of us carry that kind of power in our hands?

That's not just efficiency.

That's equity.

But here's the deeper truth: it didn't just change what I could *do*. It changed how I could *be*. I didn't need to prove I could juggle it all anymore. I just needed to protect my energy, reclaim my time, and step into a life that didn't leave me empty. And that's when I realized—this wasn't about tech. It was about liberation. The tool helped me exit old definitions of productivity and step into a version of myself I almost forgot existed.

For me? That meant feeling unstoppable.

This isn't about replacing hustle with laziness—it's about shifting from exhaustion to efficiency. It's about reclaiming time as a form of wealth.

And once I got a taste of that? I didn't stop at AI.

I started building support around me.

Because AI can help you move faster—but the right people help you move further.

So when I partnered with a virtual assistant, everything shifted again. Not only could I be more efficient—I could expand my capacity.

If you're not sure what a virtual assistant actually does, imagine this: AI gives you the starting point, but a VA becomes your thought partner. Someone who helps organize your ideas, strengthen your systems, and actually moves things forward with you—not just for you.

When done right, it's not just support—it's strategy.

And for leaders carrying a lot—big vision, heavy responsibility, constant demands—that kind of support isn't a luxury. It's a lifeline.

I'll be sharing more about how I built that system—and how you can too—through a Virtual Assistant Playbook and additional support designed for leaders who are ready to expand without burning out.

Because the goal isn't to do more.

It's to build a life and a system that can hold more—without breaking you in the process.

VISION IN MOTION:
BUILDING SMARTER, NOT HARDER

SOUND IT OUT:

- *What roles or projects are eating up your time without giving you joy or return?*
- *What's one task you could automate, delegate, or AI-ify this week?*
- *How much more time could you reclaim by working smarter, not harder?*

Now, **go to the Vision Board Section (p. 93)**. Add an image, word, or symbol that represents ease. Not laziness—ease. Flow. Alignment. Build the life that doesn't just require your hustle but also honors your humanity.

(A quick note: what I share here is my personal experience, not professional advice. AI isn't flawless—it can hallucinate, carry bias, or mishandle private information if you're not careful. And while a virtual assistant can expand your capacity, the wrong setup, lack of clarity, or poor systems can create more confusion than support. Both tools require intention, structure, and discernment. Neither replaces professional legal, financial, or medical guidance—and neither replaces your leadership. Use them wisely—as support systems, not shortcuts.)

JOURNALING THE REFLECTION CORNER:
FROM CHAOS TO CLARITY

Let's get honest.

The lie they sold us—that productivity means exhaustion is heavy. We're no longer carrying it.

SOUND IT OUT:

- *Where am I wasting the most energy?*
- *What outdated processes am I still holding onto out of habit?*
- *What tools or systems could help me reclaim my time?*
- *Why am I afraid to ask for help—even from technology?*

SET IT DOWN:

I used to think productivity meant:

Now I define productivity as:

One task I could automate is:

With that time, I'd rather:

Here's what I want you to remember:

Your mind is brilliant, but it's not built for burnout. It's built to make. And if there's a tool out there that helps you get your joy back, breathe again, and show up more fully in your life—then, baby, use it.

I didn't just save time—I reclaimed my life. That's not cheating. That's equity. That's peace.

So build better.
Don't be afraid to let AI help.
And don't be afraid to build the kind of support around you that lets you breathe again.

And if that old voice in your head says, "Do it the hard way to prove yourself,"—that's not wisdom.

That's outdated survival mode.

Get the F$#% up out of that old thinking. Exhaustion has been living rent-free in you. It's time to evict it.

Your life is worth more than burnout.

CHAPTER VI

Vision Is a Verb

Vision isn't just something you see—it's something you *do.* Something you live. It doesn't unfold in one dramatic leap, but in a thousand little transitions that add up to transformation.

This vision board—yep, the one you're looking at—was made at a friend's birthday party in January 2021. Magazines, glue sticks, and scraps everywhere. The kind of hopeful chaos that smells like possibility. I didn't know it then, but that night I was cutting and pasting my next chapter.

At the time, life was uncertain. I had just come through a period of heavy transition and was still evolving. I needed direction, so I sat with that pile of pictures and words and chose whispers of who I might be on the other side.

WALKING THE BOARD

Small Apartments and Little Houses

By the time I was 20, I already owned a rental property. On paper, it looked good—rent coming in, a little cash flow, the kind of thing people point to and say, "You're doing it right."

But what I really craved wasn't ownership.
It was space.

Space to think.
Space to breathe.
Space to just be.

That's how I ended up in a 739-square-foot home on an acre of land. Not shiny. Not new. But mine.

Dirt under my feet. Quiet when I needed it. Life all around me.

Now? Roosters wake me. Goats trim the fence line. Chickens and community dogs walk through my yard like they pay rent.

And that little house?

It holds more freedom than any big suburban home I've ever had—because it finally gave me room to come back to myself.

Live Happily & Juve Leadership Wellness Center

"Live Happily" wasn't some cute phrase I picked out. It was a fight.

In 2021, joy felt like resistance. Like choosing it meant I had to go against everything I had been taught to endure.

I had learned how to survive.
I had mastered that.

But happiness? That was unfamiliar.
That was something I had to choose on purpose.

So I put it on the board.
Right next to "Juve."

At the time, Juve was just a word.

Something about youth.
Something about rejuvenation.
Something about becoming again.

I knew it was mine.

I just didn't fully understand what I was building yet.

I didn't know it would become a company.

I didn't know it would become a space.
I didn't know it would become a way back to myself.

But that's the thing about vision—
sometimes you don't place it because you understand it.

You place it because something in you recognizes it before you do.

Coming Back to Center

"Wellness" showed up on that board before I was well.

My mind had been under attack—depression, anxiety, burnout. Not the kind you announce. The kind you carry.

So wellness wasn't a luxury.
It was survival.

And "center"…

That was me trying to come back.

Back to myself.
Back to stillness.
Back to a version of me that wasn't constantly holding everything together while quietly falling apart.

I didn't have the language for it then.
I just knew I needed to feel whole again.

Strength and Determination

In 2022 and 2023, life stretched me in ways I wasn't sure I could survive—mentally, emotionally, and spiritually.

These weren't just words on a board. They became my posture. They carried me on the days I was tired, uncertain, and questioning everything.

They kept me showing up when there was no proof the vision would work—just a quiet knowing that I couldn't quit on myself.

Black

I glued it big and bold.
No hesitation.

For too long, I hadn't fully embraced my Blackness—not because I didn't love it, but because I hadn't claimed it out loud, on purpose.

Then one day, my kids asked me if I was White.
And that moment? It stopped me.

Not out of anger—but out of awareness.

I realized they were watching me to understand who they were.
And I hadn't given them a clear enough picture.

So I made a decision.

I wanted them to see me claim it—fully.
Proudly.
Unapologetically.
Joyfully Black.

School

Back in 2005, I said I wanted to build a school by 2025.

At the time, I thought that meant four walls.
A building. A name on the front.

But vision has a way of expanding beyond what you first imagine.

Today? I may not have built a single school…
but I've helped shape many.

I've supported districts.
Coached superintendents.
Trained principals.
Guided teachers.

I've helped build systems that will continue long after I'm gone.

And that counts.

Travel, Culture & Rest

I've always loved to travel. But through AAU sports, I started to understand why. It showed me how my love for movement and my passion for youth sports could come together—creating opportunities to support scholars not just in competition, but in their educational journeys too.

When I built this board, I didn't realize how many connections my roles and responsibilities would have—or how much they would align with that passion.

There's something about being on the road, competing, moving from place to place, that feels exciting at first. New cities. New teams. New energy. It's fun.

But if you pay attention, travel starts to teach you something deeper.

It exposes you.

To different cultures.
Different environments.
Different systems—some that develop you, and some that drain you.

And I started to notice… where you land matters just as much as how talented you are.

That's what shaped my vision of becoming a K–12 sports and education agent—not just helping athletes move, but helping them move with intention. Into spaces that actually support them, see them, and stretch them in the right ways.

Because talent without alignment will burn out just as fast as it rises.

And then there's the part nobody really talks about…

Too much movement will force your body to reset—whether you plan for it or not.

Travel is exciting.
Culture is expanding.
But without rest? It becomes exhausting.

I had to learn that for myself.

So while I was dreaming about where students and athletes could go, I also had to ask—what kind of life am I building for me?

These days, I walk a few miles before work, listen to the bayou behind my land, and actually breathe.

Because the vision was never just about movement.

It was about alignment.
It was about placement.
It was about building a life—and helping others build one—where growth doesn't come at the cost of your peace.

Healthy Investments, Grace & Master Class

Not every investment has been easy—some of them cost me a whole lot more than money.

Time. Energy. Peace.
And if I'm being real… a little bit of sanity too.

Some of those "opportunities"?
Baby, they were lessons in a business suit.

But even then… they planted something.

Seeds I didn't always recognize in the moment—
because when you're in it, it just feels like stress and "what did I sign up for?"

But now? I can see it.

Things are growing.
Things are making sense.
Things are finally bearing fruit.

And grace?

Whew. Grace has been my lifeline.

Grace for the times I moved too fast.

Grace for the times I stayed too long.
Grace for figuring it out in real time—no blueprint, no manual… just me out here doing my best and adjusting on the fly.

Because if I had waited to get it perfect?
I wouldn't have moved at all.

And I've learned—progress may look a little messy, but at least it moves.

Because this journey hasn't just been about making smart investments—it's been about learning how to live better.

And that "master class"?

It didn't come from getting it all right.

It came from messing up, learning quick, and still choosing to move forward anyway.

Veggies + The Chef

I still hate cooking.
Let's just be clear about that.

But I *love* to eat.
And not just anything—I'm talking seafood boils, crème brûlée, the kind of meals that feel like an experience, not a chore.

So one day? A chef is part of the plan.

Because I've learned something along the way… Nourishment is part of wellness too.

And if I'm going to keep pouring into others, I deserve to be poured into as well—on a plate, preferably, and seasoned right.

A House

The tiny house was just a seed.

It gave me what I needed in that season—space, quiet, and room to come back to myself.

But I've always known it wouldn't be the final version.

I still dream of a larger home.

One where I can grow old, live comfortably, and create a space that feels full—of life, of laughter, of peace.

But the vision doesn't stop with me.

Juve was never meant to be just a name or a business.

It's a feeling. A place. A reset.

I see it as a retreat—somewhere people can come to rest, reset, and remember who they are outside of the roles they carry every day. Because we all need spaces that pour back into us.

And if I've learned anything… it's that the life you're building should have room for you to live in it too.

WHAT THE BOARD TAUGHT ME

A vision board doesn't need to make perfect sense. It just has to make you move.

Sometimes you glue on "school" and end up shaping education across districts.

Sometimes you glue on "Black" and end up raising kids who see you shining in your fullness.

Sometimes you glue on "Live Happily" and realize peace means letting go of what once met your needs but never nourished your soul.

And when you finally release what drained you, you make space for what grows.

Sometimes you paste a single flower—and end up with a whole garden.

This board gave me a map—not for perfection, but for becoming.

VISION IN MOTION:
WHEN THE BOARD BECOMES THE BLUEPRINT

Your vision isn't a destination—it's a verb. It lives in the choices you make, the habits you keep, the dreams you refuse to bury.

SOUND IT OUT:

What on your board have you already claimed?
What's still in progress?
What's been sitting there just looking pretty but not pushing you?

Go to the Vision Board Section (p. 93). Add one image, one word, one lyric that represents who you're becoming. Not who they told you to be.

JOURNALING THE REFLECTION CORNER:
VISION CHECK-IN TRY THIS PROMPT:

Something I've already manifested is:

A vision I'm actively working toward is:

____

____

____

____

____

____

____

A piece of my vision that no longer fits is:

____

____

____

____

____

____

____

A new image or word I want to add is:

____

____

____

____

____

____

____

And remember—this isn't about doing it all in a year. It's about saying yes.

Yes to evolving. Yes to showing up.

Yes to dreaming—even when it feels too big.

Because vision isn't passive. Vision is a verb. So get to it.

Head over to the Journal Section (p. 103). Use this space to peel back the layers of those choices. Don't just name who you are becoming—describe how it feels to finally meet her. What is the first thing you're letting go of to make room for this new version of yourself? Write without a filter; this is where your transformation becomes real.

CLOSING CHAPTER of TOOLS

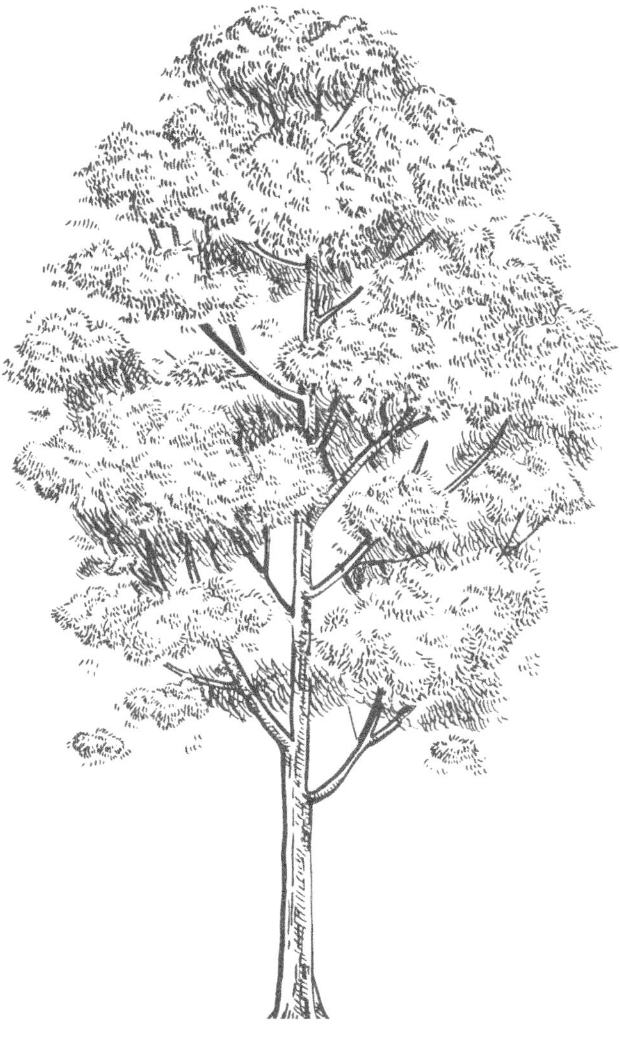

CLOSING CHAPTER AND TOOLS

You've felt the heart of the story; now it's time to use your hands. This section is your raw, unpolished starter kit—the same tactical workshop I used to cut, paste, and rebuild my life—designed to move your vision out of the "someday" drawer and into the present.

Alongside these hands-on tools, I've included an **Electronic Bonus Leadership Package** of three additional powerhouse resources specifically crafted to affirm your moves and ensure you transition from a position of authority.

Beyond the narrative, this is where the work gets real: you'll dive into the **Journal Section (p. 103)** to talk to yourself like you've got sense, use the **Vision Board Section (p. 93)** to map out the tactical details of your departure, and finally bring it all together in **Your Completed Vision (The Reality Portal, p. 119)**—a dedicated space to physically piece your vision into reality.

This entire toolkit, paired with the Bonus Leadership Package, is designed to move your dreams out of the "someday" drawer and into the present, giving you the foundation to own your truth and finally **get the f$#% up out of here**.

When It's Time To Go (For Real This Time)

Leaving isn't quitting. It isn't a weakness. It isn't disloyalty. It isn't being ungrateful.

Leaving is choosing yourself—on purpose.

And let's be clear: you can leave the room without flipping the table. You can transition gracefully and powerfully. You can bless folks and still block their access. You can say, "Thank you for the lesson," and still sprint in the opposite direction. Because if alignment ain't there, your assignment ain't either.

I used to think grace was soft like bubble baths and quiet time. Now I know grace is fierce. Grace is that voice that says: "Girl, you already gave your all. And that's enough."

Grace is pausing when you'd rather push. It's letting go before life snatches it from your hands. It's deciding to be whole, even if that means being somewhere else.

Timing doesn't always come with an RSVP. Sometimes you don't know you overstayed until your body breaks down. Until your kid says, "You never smile anymore." Until your therapist raises an eyebrow and asks, "So what are we doing here?"

But when is it time? Baby, it's time. Pack up your peace. Grab your boundaries. Leave the emotional leftovers. And go. Because truthfully? You don't owe anyone your peace. But you owe yourself the truth.

Starter Kit: Tools to Get You Moving

Let me pause here. Everything you just read? That was the heart. But inspiration only goes so far if it isn't paired with action. That's why I've included these tools—not for later, but for now.

They're here so you can start where you are, while the ideas are fresh, before life tries to tuck them away in the "someday" drawer. Think of this as your starter kit—the same kinds of tools I leaned on while cutting, pasting, crying, and rebuilding.

They're not polished for Instagram—they're messy, personal, and honest.

I've condensed these so you have something in your hands right away. The full extras—templates, guides, and bonus tools—live in the digital bundle. But this right here? It's more than enough to get you moving.

If you want to go deeper, that next layer is waiting for you. Consider this your warm-up—the rest is where your vision really starts to grow legs.

Soundtrack for Your Exit Anthems for Power Moves:

- "Break My Soul" – Beyoncé
- "Golden" – Jill Scott
- "Bag Lady" – Erykah Badu
- "Level Up" – Ciara
- "Unstoppable" – Sia

Songs That Got Me Through the Exit:

- "I'm Leaving" – Mary J. Blige
- "Energy" – Beyoncé
- "I Hope You Dance" – Lee Ann Womack
- "Freedom" – Jon Batiste
- "I'm Moving On" – Rascal Flatts

Journal Prompts:
Talk to Yourself Like You Got Sense! What's Trying to End Itself?

I've been dragging my feet because:

But honestly, I already know:

The lie I keep telling myself is:

What I actually need is:

My Exit Strategy (In Progress):

I'm making room for:

One thing I'm no longer explaining is:

A boundary I'm about to put in place is:

The version of me I'm becoming says:

TRANSITION CHECKLIST: "AM I IN OR JUST SCARED TO LEAVE?"

Answer honestly. No judgment. Just clarity.

- ☐ My body feels safe here.
- ☐ I can be my whole self here.
- ☐ I don't shrink or censor to survive.
- ☐ I see growth that excites me—not just tolerable progress
- ☐ I'm not staying just because it's familiar.

If fewer than three checked? You're not stuck—you're settling.

Leaving is not about quitting—it's about choosing yourself on purpose. Whether your next move is blasting Beyoncé in the car, scribbling in a journal, or finally cutting out that vision board image you've been staring at for months, remember:

You don't owe anyone your peace. You owe yourself your freedom.

So if you need permission to leave, hear my loud voice and get the F$#% up out of there.

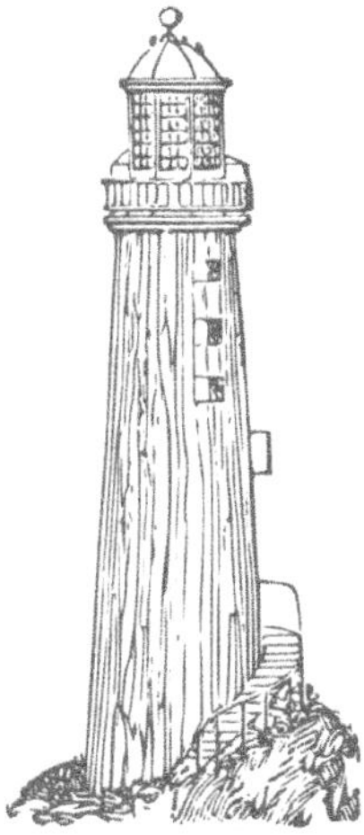

GET THE F$#% UP OUT OF HERE

VISION BOARD

Your vision needs a home—give it a place to live right here so you can see your evolution every single day.

INTRODUCTION:

Jot three images/words that pull you forward right now.

CHAPTER I

Where in your current work are you pretending everything is fine, but your soul knows otherwise? Are you performing for others while quietly abandoning yourself? What would a work life in complete alignment with your values, family needs, and spiritual peace actually look like? What's one shift—slight or bold—that would bring you closer to a more authentic version of you?

CHAPTER II

Add an image, a quote, or a color that represents leadership on your terms. This isn't about climbing the ladder. It's about building a ladder no one thought to make.

CHAPTER III

Add a word, an image, a song lyric—whatever pulls you toward your next place of becoming. This is your blueprint. Not for what others expect of you, but for who you're allowed to be when no one else is scripting your life.

CHAPTER IV

Add one word or image that represents freedom without fear—the version of your financial future built by you, not just for you.

CHAPTER V

Add an image, word, or symbol that represents ease. Not laziness—ease. Flow. Alignment. Build the life that doesn't just require your hustle but also honors your humanity.

CHAPTER VI

What on your board have you already claimed? What's still in progress? What's been sitting there just looking pretty but not pushing you? Add one image, one word, one lyric that represents who you're becoming. Not who they told you to be.

GET THE F$#% UP OUT OF HERE

JOURNAL

Own your truth and talk to yourself like you've got sense—it's time to bleed your next chapter onto these pages.

THE REALITY PORTAL:
Your Completed Vision

Bring the visions from each chapter together to see the full picture of your future; now, the only step left is to carry this clarity back into your reality and start the work you already know how to do.

Made in the USA
Coppell, TX
12 June 2026

81469884R00075